SWIMMING

poems by

Barbara Flug Colin

Finishing Line Press
Georgetown, Kentucky

SWIMMING

Copyright © 2020 by Barbara Flug Colin
ISBN 978-1-64662-291-7 First Edition
All rights reserved under International and Pan-American Copyright Conventions. No part of this book may be reproduced in any manner whatsoever without written permission from the publisher, except in the case of brief quotations embodied in critical articles and reviews.

ACKNOWLEDGMENTS

Special thanks to Arthur Vogelsang.

Publisher: Leah Maines

Editor: Christen Kincaid

Cover concept: Simon Usdan

Cover design: Grace Hopkins: www.gracehopkins.squarespace.com

Order online: www.finishinglinepress.com
also available on amazon.com

Author inquiries and mail orders:
Finishing Line Press
P. O. Box 1626
Georgetown, Kentucky 40324
U. S. A.

*For Fred,
and for our family,
always*

storm inside first wave burst
darkness

foaming eye of shoreline
loosening more rungs from slivered silver horizon

beginning swim parallels right left
harmonizing body recomposing sea

as tightly laced cave darkness
hibernates vehemently
*

aren't you swimming parallels to shore summer air then there
without this line to circuit here inside this paneled shadowed velvet light you are

swimming in winds designing rivulets inside wave arcs
breaking over you on your back

swimming from too far back
out below sky canopy of red streaming irrationally

suspended over veiled walls
closing in darkness encroaching to see

whole too deep in your nature
you first were swimming toward a foreign land

to contain wave intensity
*

surface dive into dawn lake
slide glide through frigid solution

to depth darkness is
anything reduced to itself
*

swim underwater aware of drop, currents, rocks
emerge in form childhood disciplined

body breaks
into its strokes
*

*I am always tackling something impossible
up from pond bottom* Monet said
*

time beginning green undulations seen
through transparent surface light waves

up from my source
*

my beginning ocean
and Seine

I channeled
into Giverny
*

she said *baba stop*

paddling so I did so we sat in summer sun in a calm inlet
as she patted thick green almost circular lily pads
*

pushing pulling thundering pain contracting
mother I replace

pushing pushing with
in cyclone rhythm
I see my newborn's tiny face

hind in rear view
framing thundering cry
*

pushing pushing
one arm floats sinks

in rhythm with other arm spoke wheeling palms
opening to finger sea swimming through your

narrow dawn brook center
to circle whole lake to locks unlocking new lakes

leveling each other
to brook river

past the waterfall to downstream hurricane-filled depth
of still original

bluewhite skysea back country
*

mom I never before understood
nursing her newborn

I watch the monitors
*

your body bearing awe full thaw
temperature rise

facing sun
feeling then now in its own rhythmic kick

backstroke wheeling forward unreeling mind
elides into gelid solution

left elbow right knee equivalence with nothing but this whole
well oiled automatic machine provides free ride
*

moon tides beginning currents wave doesn't want to be
first sea desires desiring more

father where were you
far out first wave stirred moon too distant to measure the first pull
*

your brook rushing brushing underbelly pushing pulling
determined up streams down
as foliage protects pained reservoir moisture
*

your sea galloping free
reined
halts bolts bursts

third eye

to see deepest origin signed
etched in stone wall
beyond the basement pane
*

your square glass room remains
on sea bottom to see from all sides
coming
*

a block from home bouldered our first sea fenced in concrete
we climbed searching unafraid for unknown hitler we
were sure hid inside boulder holes
*

so we were driven to swim in the next Brighton Beach
real 45 foot high waves brother said

we were 4 and 5 and trusted our paired race across
the elemental desert toward the promised

sea returning remembered solvency
before need to survive overwhelming wave bankruptcy
*

she said *baba stop paddling* so I did so we sat in summer sun in a calm inlet
as she patted thick green almost circular lily pads

baba I am learning...

moving shadows below pond surface
*

letters to paint our forest white shaping screens
circle dancing inside squares dancing pairs tarring roads
for more vehicles to pound sound

rushing brook brushes under wooden bridge
water falls vibrates belly smell pushes pull downstream

not knowing it is determined up streams down

foliage protects pained reservoir moisture

thought shadows flight of white winged darkness
*

wave center arched fell styling soul creating
new kicks bends rhythms

to shape this darkness in depth to dive in
to retrieve it before she

dried the waves
*

first wave reined halted bolted rose fell
shatter any body keeps

returning to familiar inside this hourglass *I will make myself
my own pool* Matisse said and stilled motion in spaced shaped
*

beginning sea shadowed by sun
scarred by reflection pulsating sensation

trained framed mirrored self-reflecting shifting clouds
resolving aqueous planes of dissolution without time

to return to safe ground to keep discovering
I remained the same I need you to be across

to feel being
other sides of sea

I am first
swimming
*

us cross country east west speeding north south down hills too steep to stop
sliding across iced highways to find ourselves on expressways

driven out to find this
longest bridge suspended
motion midway midlife
in the middle of our country

this vastness of body below
and necessity for each to reach each other

tests courage to get to another side
of darkness trolled bouldered

wild beast
tamed

in images first illustrated in childhood pages turning turning from
emptiness into an empty store

for a proprietor entering to sweep the floor
for another coming to build shelves for other

ingredients for greater feasts
obscuring pure scared scarred darkness

coming to light nothing coming to form
animal to be paired for the flood coming

to keep it in wooden ark arched cathedral flooding needing more design for
the circling intensity of body broken

curves straightened to starve the animal inside concrete pockmarked room
apart

apartment above a carless garage
for children to act out in play memorized roles
*

driving across the longest bridge surprised to find ourselves now here in time
being alive

to discover this human disease
we are

this terror always being trained safe tracked grounded engined responsible
containers

of possibility pounding on the door awakening to be shored grounded desire
desiring more
*

longing for the apple dangling and body below reaching to be
sea we are

driving us across this endless bridge and you know to manipulate the
wheeling one arm spoke in rhythm with the other

slightly too far out right or left
to crash the fence like the child did

choosing never to be stitched back in
and feeling disabled by such a slight incursion

stored whole now with the wheel to control impossible infinity of sea to be
suspended across then now seen scene stilled real

empty identity disembodied bridged freed reality in time
sifted through the hourglass

stalled familiar to see inside childhood booked
*

and the stores as simple as a child's drawing and not hard to get to be in
swimming the river we are

swimming 'til mom says *get out in one cigarette*
time spent watching white form her breath

white being burned down
*

which of my drawings do you like best baba

don't ask another you know more

I don't draw at all he said
then suddenly it comes

what makes it come baba
*

darkness is
finding forms

discovering
himself
*

in ramshackle dead Monet's ignored stacked dusty Giverny
young Ellsworth Kelly uncovers in forgotten paintings or recreates

in real rail shadows on his rented steps down to the beach
or up to his balcony or outside in streetlight shadowing

inner white wall to his rented basement
darkness

he recreates his relief hung small portable from a French ceiling
to return home upstate New York to recreate real animal descent

from his hills *deer come down like crazy* to be steel
self reflective sun blocked giant sculpture shadows

shaping the darkness
on his mown lawn
*

shadowed steps down to sea
shadowed steps up to balcony

shadow racing toward steps up from basement
torsoed shadow escaping in ascent out west
*

driving us across this endless suspension
too frightened to look down to see reality of sea
*

learning increased safety inside moving sound coming to shape darkness
synthetic white eye tracked trained to stand being hit then exploring alternates

to be all sides
of the reservoir before waterfall shored blanketed infant fling kick
*

stored green mown before memory trained the dream seen from higher
cheaper seats for center conflict being played out in stadium center court

*

in a hearing in the basement we hear reproductions of hunger we appease
cooking or when it's not enough

taking them out or imagining we do and they are patient
and abide inside or seem to join on the diagonal plain

on which our home resides
a plane on an angle for the viewer to see going out west

would be easy if we are patient being
suspended inside this awful drive across not knowing what is an other side
*

nights below the boulders and flapping back to trauma and what it is and if it
was the child pleading pleading to return to darkness inside

the room whose storied wallpaper could have several titles with its black
background bursting pink blossoming as it climbs

and the silence terrible in its antipathy seeming to try to let in
sounds playing punchball kickball out on the street

where no cars interfered within the child pushing pulling pressing
to finally answer or analyze or discover or make known some

newly retrieved same unknown in darkness below
all the rolling vehicles not yet understood down inside

the basement room drawing left inside
scattered shattered talent-quick furry pencil lines

trying to contour partial foliage protected scenes of unseen palpable
dimensional sensuous whole then
*

in a hammock by the Saugatuck river
the sound of the fall and the sign of the sunned white strands

seeming like icicles sometimes parting like glass
hair uncover grayed right angled stone dam

the thin door opens
and a wisp of river air smells like childhood

can be contained

the river exhales its cool warmth
just a breath

then the heat closes the porthole
*

then we were driven from the waves through Brighton Beach
streets in darkness below the el suspended above our car

daddy was driving me inside stopped in the dream
to see the reality of the bridge suspended tracked trains coming

from deepest in Brooklyn
*

walking across the first wooden footbridge above Sheepshead Bay
learning to read the sign *do not make fast to this bridge*

we left home to get across this to the illicit frightening
unkosher white flesh shelled red we cracked and sucked
*

how far have we come
how far is there to go

to return to same
animal center home
*

basement walls scathed yellow
floor clean white still

except for excerpts
of the bird

feathers strewn
one bulb dangling from the ceiling
*

some figure achieved of generation in two Torah sides unscrolling
and this movie begins or will soon but where to sit as the room edits itself
*

you left home to cross this bridge left to right to be in this vehicle you are

driving wandering wondering where does all this lead
and outside below you can see your ancestors paired divided to

easily be edited whole O swimming sea
*

endlessly
suspended

afraid
to look down
*

desperate

Matisse painted his *bonheur de vivre* eden
to return to the left

to choose any subject to shape color if your soul styles it that way
any subjective accretion of eden then all the accretions can be

contained concentric circles waiting for some
body to return from war to let out the hulled smell

and the sound of the fall
of real material
*

and these are the accretions language provides
concentric circles within *I*

don't discover I
recover Miro said
*

turns returning loosening strokes
leaking secrets of facets of light in JMW Turner's fury

at his mother's fury in his watercolor
more interested in ruins than in archeology
*

I did something night scary
I called for you
I went out into the unlit hall alone
I pursued a clue
I called help or something else then
I helped myself maybe you

that's all there was
screamed words
scarred feared alike difference
related rhymes since dissonance
as just relics to call out for
others or any gear to engine

vehicles resenting first
language so primitive it was shared by all
way before babel
way before brothers twinned bad good
way before wave deluged
ark saved your animal
paired in garden before
two beady eyes slithering wordless sting
and the apple dangling
and body below just out of reach
of fruitful branching hung
before being plucked
color from light to name spectrum
*

not raw rotted thawed
fresh raw
*

as the shadow finally pursuing you

but you resisted repulsed
but lead him on
but understood

the real is today unshaded now here this huge bridge
your private being crossed with other people in their cars
and your children want to cross too in their metaphors
*

the reality you taught reading them the same books to see reality is this
illustrated cow on another side

that boulders first
this

illustrated first page of a cow
is facing ahead beside the red facade
*

did the child know why the cow is outside the red barn
and the scene is frozen inside the book

or that the barn dreams of diagonals
to feel potential extension to keep more and more inside

does the cow know it was once shaped animal purity now
white polka dotted by misshapen black

islands of darkness
echoing to each other I need more land

not to be crossing this endlessness
by being

not being recreated deconstructed in time
by a Von Doesburg and Mondrian cow abstracting

to discover meaning of the animal drowned inside
facade symbol

to feel the cow could look forward to being inside what is concrete walled
room apart

for black and white to recover each other
as red recovers animal yearning to expand

to contain possibility of loss

in childhood

of infant infinity
needing a cross
*

to the reservoir
you biked to in summer air

and fell on wet tar
as he biked over your thighs

feeling black and blue being
tracked
*

we left the old country habits
and ancestors' homes burned and robbed

now old towns drowned inside
this neighborhood
*

children playing without knowing how to drive across this bridge
of possibilities of infestations of insects clinging to inner walls

as if forming patterns or signs of darkness
protruding like disease for the child in danger of falling again

the water increasing
waves rising

determined for immersion in emergent sea
to make you see what is
*

inside right in time to get there to swim or lie naked on anyone not tempted
sure of your intention of yourself of need to be

with no one in particular or do what anyone else expects wants designs
what hasn't even begun or is going on

as imperfect

and chaotic as your left home
*

to get across to right now here safe looking down
from this porch or looking from this side of the river or

looking from behind the iron fence we biked to the reservoir
first falling then closer to here further from there

looking down acrophobic from this mountain edge
as grooved rock erosion trickle sifts streaming descent
*

or looking upstream beyond blocking boulders
that stopped our kyacks before the cart

bridge before looking down from this porch
to this waterfall so far beyond first burst

naked newborn armfling leg swim
shored this far downstream from the reservoir

that grass is already mown
*

                swimming parallels

Being taught, I feel conceiving
body curves, embodying sensuous

Hebrew letters, English letters
my eyes up here see distanced out
side body, closest, relatives, in words

named parents, siblings, anybody else is not
self, el in the name of Evelyn, Samuel, Helene,
Ellwyn and Elohim above all else.
*

First is home, or person, or neighborhood Brooklyn took
brook for first country home on Easton Road is in Westport, in Connect I cut,
like basement, attic, down up, east west north south…or anything you say is

in body,

my first drive I am driven from Manhattan Beach, to Brighton Beach, two, I am,
learning where darkness is below tracked elevated steel
moving sound parallels shadowed below the Brighton Beach el,

until Coney Island, third out in sun
light recreates el in Carousel, Wonder
Wheel, Steeplechase…

like first parallel to sea
is blocks away in final beginning Stillwell Station trains coming going,
forward back, like time

I am learning to tell, my life in my diary mommy dictates to me,
as I am learning to write both ways
English and Hebrew like the Stillwell trains.
*

   …but it was so juicy and I lay below the drip drip drip from the center…
*

You are, familiar, my, second character, in the first room I am,
inside, looking out through panes of my eyes,
like room windows framed, like a painting hung inside on a wall,

with same figures rushing forward or back,
so am I in or out, rushing to or from
a feeling of leaving returning animal reined

dreaming rain forms this umbrella language is
in memory of seeing out pane, eye is, second person seen
waiting room of memory retained body feeling falling

failing being inside awaiting room feeling
disconnected from seen learned being
distanced in a room apart from painful beginning

being distanced self from even now as I am remembering
so I don't know if what I saw was even further out scene
in memory of same many rush hour men in homburgs

under their black umbrellas all

same diagonally leaning right
rushing home at dusk
*

so many men to fill the dream
in my family history men model best perfect
so I choose men models as my story stays still

mystery of my own being s/he forming
fe/male protected solution to the fall I could not feel
under their umbrella so could I really be

live or have
my own original
forming me to feel it

being formed to stand withstanding

I am beginning to understand I am what I am
that I am not them or mom or you or anybody else
*

not Matisse's first child he paints over in his first dining room painting
receiving the solution poured by the Breton servant Matisse is
looking for a self deeper in body

in third dining room he cut
a left window out to pink house furthest from the room
of red intensity wall papered table clothed in flowering eyes secure

in viewing your Coney Island voyeur displaced body vehicles recreating your
wonder wheeling cyclone circling on precipice edge of skysea Matisse paints
next broken circle then his late fragile last cut out space body equivalence

balanced composed precarious threatening to fall
inside his dining room wall
inside the MoMA burlap wall
*

the dream museum provides first
red train leaving first station
to be inside vehicle of emotion

tracked being trained engineless
then engined to look out to see what leaving is
what moving means

what stays inside same
red feeling being blanketed hidden
blocked out in language
*

Deep in, below
the Brighton Beach el,
in second neighborhood person,

a stop on my memory mapped a clue of leaving home for an adult dream
of the reality of the el I return to see the real final tracked body curve left
before the el

trains stayed the same moving on
to Coney Island out in open sun.
The el vanishing.
*

…juicy delicious under belly drip drip pee snot sap honeysuckle center
ooze…across   from…
          …umbilical   axed next
                    from   yum yum…
*

Sea waves cave.
Interior cyclone whirling cylinder
tunnels darkness.
Bearing first being is.

Becoming. Form rises, inhales, whinnies on hind.
Height suspended fell. Shatter shored dried repeats.
Dark light flight height fall foam push pull feel
disappearance first being beached bouldered. Hid hitler.
*

circling Matisse dancers reaching hands can't hold on
figures galloping toward you are reined
ringed animal explodes
third eye wakes

meaning missed
until this glassed collapsed beached hidden hitler I was
improper unpunctuated naughty blame
excited what means hitler? why angry elohim exterminates

idols
hollow
echoed clawed white dark
arced interior sounds
*

Only I in my family home kiss mezuzahs by every door
like we are all supposed to.

Then parents and we five children walk one block from home a different way
than to the beach.

The bay we cross is a Sheepshead. The other side is another kind of L.
Unkosher L u n d y s.

They, sucking cracking red shells.
I a girl eat chicken so am I or they to blame.
*

is this how pull dies
why never silence any more
why there is always war
am I criminal or saviour
*

pretend there is a long narrow cardboard box
randomly placed in the Stillwell station

and inside is a less long narrow cardboard box
and inside is a less long silver rod

to defuse the rifle
and the train is due on time

what am I to do
defuse the gun or make the train

save the day or even lives

or take the gun and get away with crime

am I the caterer cooking time to appease this hunger
or out of time unsatiated sensuous naked

appetite to rape some figure
of language or imagination

for generations to admit
I am two sides

of a Torah unscrolling
or many chairs in many rooms and I don't know which side to sit on

and I forgot the tix to watch the movie flapping back to trauma or what it is
and if it was pleading pleading to return to darkness I knew before I became

the room
of storied wallpaper of any of several titles

with its black background bursting pink
blossoming as it climbs to let in sound from out on Exeter Street

where no cars interfere with our punch ball game
so we can't get run over

as sound discovers some
newly retrieved same

unknown darkness in a basement room left
scattered shatter inside exfoliating foliage

to protect scenes unseen palpable dimensional
as the bald shadow pursues me and I resist repulsed

but lead him on
and the huge pool available in shade fills

with people and my daughter wanting to swim
and the shock of husbands coming

to exonerate wives sex excesses
and all the obfuscation of metaphor earned

immersion for emergence sea
and its barnacles
*

and then
our disappointment in the room

how could this be us
how to take flight not forgot the tix
how to stop the apartment from filling with water

why does ancestor on floor conflate converse participate
why not open gifts of rooms of possibilities of infestations coming
why are insects clinging to wall forming patterns or signs to clean up room

advancing from private to public
despite embolism
despite all floors or two we enter

despite her child in danger of chaos and mess and water increase
inside reports of degrees unrelated I
leave red orange leaves
*

arched bark revealing peeling
second floor terror of illicit
so I know how to code

evade shame pain blame
knotting page by page
exposed human faced

participated in familial engaged rage
descending to pathology
armored zombies all the same

stuffing formed cellophaned
to appear disclaimed embarrassment closed down
like infected public pool
*

imperfections defects change style opening to
any swimmers cellophaned armored discombobulated

trapped bodies hidden in form to name

this pathology it was
just another exercise to exorcize cardboard cliché family stories
persistent residents to hide

the sap you named the only taste I knew then
not the cardboard stage set finally collapsed
but the push to pull center stamen
*

not to get more or less but just that or this one
drop from your
center
*

from inner first circle pond
forested darkness before

branching metaphors to look for
or
*

the ordinary that is interred because it was then
from before now concentric circles

of the impossible
length of the bridge suspended

to carry the driver's drive back
to the first shore

bouldered by simple illustrations in memory
of memories to stay then now
*

simple origin
seen scene

first architecture built in
your nature

separated from its animal

a to z just a

simple cow
a red faced house exuding future red barn extended by diagonals white cow was
pierced intruded by residues of darkness it grew out of
*

the drive is a surprise as if you are being driven doing research in the back seat
but no you are driver you realize as you see sides right left ahead below and
in the rear view you are driving from across endless sea you are inside
*

so many sides of solution to parents siblings or your generations
you must sustain this
suspension a coke can placed between your legs is

a miniature to feel where you are and that you can
squeeze your two sides together to feel
the intermediary mediating
*

to keep going on the impossible narrow endless bridge in the center of states
now united if you can seam them by this dry drive and not veer
toward another fall over the side
*

can you feel ending in the beginning without troll to control to approach
the fear of your other you are out without you
to complete

original
without competition
to land home without blocks or scene seen
*

just you beginning forming
unknown untaught home
animal milk sucked pure white
*

without residue darkness
forming moving felt
without memory window

framed still scene sequestered
child before drawing scene
inside drawn from seen sign designed
by taught forms

never willing to connect the dots
or paint advocated red barn
green lawn black and white animal
your own owned drive
in states united untitled in
members spanning time
to buoy sea
*

until red is facaded white poked black holes in whole darkness to picket white
fenced forming animal skinned meaning of feeling in time in the dream
we felt we were alone inside this amiss messed chaos us
to hide in conventional cellophane inflated same form
*

bridged glimpses of sea below surface being pushed or pulled
from below sea to illustrate pulsing in more basic signs of reality
of shimmering stacatto sparked dark bolts electric
wave arch whinnies of fall embodied shored bouldered all
*

displaced from wooden one room cabin to trailer
moving forward to being
labelled on bottle necks

better than carbonated colored in can
cannot be bottled pure
currents currency to

party but is this
new resort the best
is each bite each activity each meal each move

better than the rest who move into our space for us
regardless of I
let out
*

at night
in dark streets of bad neighborhoods or
unfinished

or gentrifying to good
moving in unknown directionless dissed
spelling burst

relieved to feel
unknown
pressure let out

in unknown darkness
uncaring about danger
or unremembered friends lower less successful then now
*

welding me in if only if only I don't impose old valued attitudes ingrown
feat of no matter how much effete richness must serve a proper feast
of deepest horizon thin iridescence caught
*

told in just a page turned or filled blackboard rolled
into a new blank canvas
but it was there

I felt it told
but
unfelt revived I

felt it asserting assertive proof of existence but
unabsorbed object like all those other lines crossing other pages
to enclose j'accuse
*

hitler hiding in boulders
*

thinking I can keep it hidden if I tell her to hide
and they too are accused more publicly more viable

mine can be kept secret and as I swim sweet I show them why
I am how I am if I am seen

I am proof of their accusation

while others are found
out as if in this accusation of sin
is a cause visible

as smoke or seditious scent
or actual smell
or targets of fate of fall

of first cause
of guilt
of this unknown done
*

is my center my bullseye I must hide my white strip inside
some vulnerability stadium outside by first sea
holes boulders not big enough to enter

some shame something hidden
so I hide inside my rock stacked castle moated
by oncoming sea shored by me
*

never guilt sin unforgiven
the young ogle at
us

waiters bearing silver round trays stacked with red treif
shells betray the untitled we feel we are entitled to flesh
we know how to title
*

the once unemployed inexperienced
to see into
for those about to know what

was your greatest success
grouped excerpts like us
but different in need

or worse off
new idea of I

to be or do or go but waiting for service
*

from first beached shored
dawn horizon plain plane fresh
as any fresh start as

child/mother bearing child
born/borne bearer/bare
mother bearing cub

father tide/moon/entombed
in womb determined
mother determining rhythms cohering
*

as sea determined by tide
as waves as rise
as fall determined

enwombed bearing being entombed
as solution bearing beginning being women form as
paned room to contain bearing pains rhythmic

tide abides by
breathing inoutin its
rhythms
*

to get it out as worst pain bears best form of you to be born as form growing
in solution coming to form

waves of pain demanding you conform in rhythm you are not
the stallion you are dreaming or recreating from the seen
*

you are I
in their image but not

yet seen but felt inside only one body you are
requiring to be a team in this

worst pain of birth to immerse in these contractions you feel the iced scar undefined as yet no such word just

tides moon pull push aqueous being formed fetus you were
and now are a part in form a part of sea coming to form

rising falling shattered by shores to be coming
forming swimming

inside designated shaped first and last
resort being seen or not

being inside body feeling being
embodied until somebody else familial

but not family just challenge to identity except then accept ability to change
die revive differently succeeding in reverence of is

envy mer is sea finally
revived in formed

somebody else to relate or relate to feel being seen show
showing something you must be but don't feel until being revered

by iterations of caretakers of her
offspring or any other solution water =
*

waiting
there are laws
can't be aggressive

relatives know and go before
there is an order
then

you discover
it already occurred
you

don't remember
the train or training or how or what the seats or window views were you
are there to discover and decide whether this pregnancy is doable and

then if this second is too late or
late like your mother so you'll match her or can't
and must abort so much earned

will have to be shared so much
concentration will have to be
spread less

care for more offspring
and where are the children who left
their shoes at the threshold of the first room in time I am

entering myself watching her wondering about them and I
wonder how far she gets
inside the room though it is so small and alone as no other room has yet been
built for many stories she is it or I here watching her entering the room

watching her fulfill my expectation that she has already crossed to the center
and felt the solubility of the walled room the child left to get to the left she
cannot return to as she
worries about their shoelessness and their nakedness
*

though already having entered their existence
the disappearance of the room that seemed the first stage set
props of shoes almost describable
or at least she wants to narrate them as *unlaced*
*

though maybe they were never even worn and the memory of the children
she was longing for
was simply an object of desire desiring more objects to retrieve
to remind members to remember somebody she had been
*

many already
I had perhaps waited for
as I had to but

the rules and characters of waiting
the line and bench to sit on
the emotion of defiance of then

submission to inevitability yet
the travel details
and the hole I was sure was the train I was to wait for and
*

yet there I was
here inside
and people vague but palpable

familial and surprise even excitement acceptance of this late
pregnancy then ambivalence about yet
another offered implanted that

particular sunlight seen from drive
vehicled going toward that
unmediated

sun firing
white
concrete
*

fading correct lifts away
finally it recurs
the empty rooms

the promised party
no food drinks
nothing expected

their disappointment
mine in what I was
what I couldn't do to fill the rooms with what was
*

expected and their compromised acceptance of what they were
leaving to unite and go to be done in truth
memory is

only available clue
cue symbol sign sea unravels
waves exhausted rest in sand
*

dry die relive this
current sea revived
past time inside the hourglass

for future genealogy of some
body in pastime I am something
outside of me

being
a good sport
playing myself out in it
*

diving for precious ancient lure real
feathers woods
guarded

withstood beside the original
not understanding
being drowned

disconnected tree they axed from roots
the pair left interred across
just a small space

but the longest distance from here
to for there for the
beginning

to build the bridge with words symbols signs
any material to suspend vehicles
that will not fall
*

pod covered recovered
shells hardened
color darkened in time

red to black to get back
darkness
itself
*

                              I just had this little thing to say
this small resonate podded from then
                         this seed essence shelled by el

these simple child feelings
            or views tastes smells tiny from this distance inside this vehicle
engines fast forward down steep hills
*

safely brakeless cross country without police
                                        trying to find what is
hidden buried so far back in pastime
*

as original as endangered flesh shelled red
black coming back threatening to find hidden I

was determined didn't choose I
simply dove down easily didn't need clues to cue it and I

magnetized by each
other so no directive no direction no map no sign no vibration

someday I'd hatch that sea weed pod
that held the sea from then

in time I return it
to itself
*

but finally across sea bouldered so I could fall more safely
from lower in the arch crescendo

but I did not let go
I did not need my drive ahead to see what is

coming across the desert
to be the present I

looked to my right
left beside the bridge to see then
*

a scene simple as my first construction
of home yellow-complected blue-eyed wood facade

reflected composite of my mirrored face and mask
of taught symbol

red lipped closed door to this too a home
with the wild beast already excluded
*

white pocked
black pure light
*

breaks through from darkness coming to
scar the white cow

with irregular imperfect growing out of her
darkness was the strength of it all
*

in a scene I turned my face to see a page torn
from childhood as it was

no longer my own
but owned by the
*

then restaurants to mark shore
relatives to arrive

random participation in randomly eating from all
or any available all l named can

able wanting contacts
to remain repeats
*

dead memorable characters' remains of the day
pain formed her

deformed convention to unmask her
start from necessity already as a child she was

grown twin concomitant luxuriously dependent on dependence
on poverty of richness parallels tried to feed each

other to endure but remain
personal help to each
*

like I is in
swimming

in time it
got in fiction

built the bridge
words are

to replace lost
center

                                                                                     I am swimming

shored stored shelved selves accruing what else
how many bodies

of water must I cross to free primitive
that

froze
to be

kept
at bay
*

gently incise the thin skin
pull the tender stamen

empty center
to taste

its
one sweet drop
*

*baba can't you see
Monet didn't care that it
was named*

haystack

*he just liked its shape its colors
its textures
in changing light*

www.ingramcontent.com/pod-product-compliance
Lightning Source LLC
LaVergne TN
LVHW040117080426
835507LV00041B/1283